W9-BNO-329

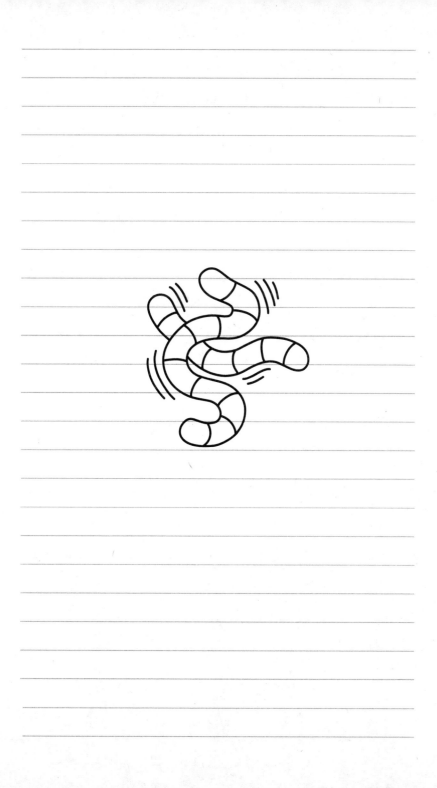

Other Books by Jeff Kinney

Diary of a Wimpy Kid

Diary of a Wimpy Kid: Rodrick Rules

Diary of a Wimpy Kid: The Last Straw

Diary of a Wimpy Kid: Dog Days

Diary of a Wimpy Kid: The Ugly Truth

Diary of a Wimpy Kid: Cabin Fever

Diary of a Wimpy Kid: The Third Wheel

Diary of a Wimpy Kid: Hard Luck

Diary of a Wimpy Kid: The Long Haul

Diary of a Wimpy Kid: Old School

Diary of a Wimpy Kid: Double Down

DIARY
of a
Wimpy Kid
DOUBLE DOWN

BY JEFF KINNEY

THORNDIKE PRESS
A part of Gale, Cengage Learning

GALE
CENGAGE Learning

Farmington Hills, Mich • San Francisco • New York • Waterville, Maine
Meriden, Conn • Mason, Ohio • Chicago

GALE
CENGAGE Learning®

Thorndike Press, a part of Gale, Cengage Learning.

Thorndike Press® Large Print Mini-Collections.
The text of this Large Print edition is unabridged.
Other aspects of the book may vary from the original edition.
Set in 16 pt. Plantin.

LIBRARY OF CONGRESS CATALOGING-IN-PUBLICATION DATA

Names: Kinney, Jeff, author, illustrator.
Title: Diary of a wimpy kid : double down / by Jeff Kinney.
Other titles: Double down
Description: Waterville, Maine : Thorndike Press, 2017. | "Thorndike Press
    Large Print Mini-Collections"—Copyright page. | Originally published in a
    slightly different form by Amulet Books in 2016. | Summary: Greg Heffley's
    mom wants him to take a break from video games while Halloween
    approaches and he comes up with an idea to make a movie.
Identifiers: LCCN 2016053566| ISBN 9781410498687 (hardback) | ISBN
    1410498689 (hardcover)
Subjects: LCSH: Large type books. | CYAC: Diaries—Fiction. | Family life—
    Fiction. | Motion pictures—Production and direction—Fiction. | Halloween—
    Fiction. | Humorous stories. | Large type books. | BISAC: JUVENILE FICTION /
    Humorous Stories. | JUVENILE FICTION / Comics & Graphic Novels / General.
Classification: LCC PZ7.K6232 Dht 2017 | DDC [Fic]—dc23
LC record available at https://lccn.loc.gov/2016053566

Published in 2017 by arrangement with Amulet Books an imprint of
Harry N. Abrams, Inc.

TO DORIAN

Wednesday

My parents are always saying the world doesn't revolve around me, but sometimes I wonder if it actually DOES.

When I was a little kid, I saw this movie about a man whose whole life is secretly being filmed for a TV show. This guy is famous all over the world, and he doesn't KNOW it.

Well, ever since I saw that movie, I've kind of figured the same thing is probably happening to ME.

At first I was annoyed my life was being broadcast without my permission. But then I realized that if millions of people are tuning in every day to see what I'm up to, that's actually kind of COOL.

Sometimes I worry that my life is too BORING to be its own television show, so I try to do something entertaining every now and then to give the people watching at home a good chuckle.

The other thing I do is send my audience little signals to let them know I'm in on the secret.

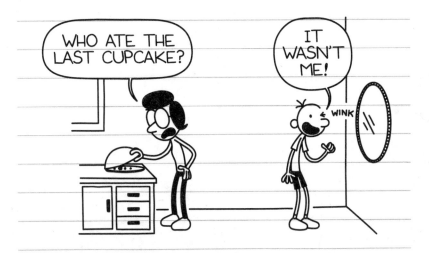

If my life's a TV show, then there's gotta be commercial breaks. I figure they must run the ads when I'm in the bathroom, so I always make a big entrance after I finish up in there.

But sometimes I wonder how much of my life is REAL and how much of it is RIGGED. Because half the things that happen to me are so ridiculous, I wonder if someone ELSE is pulling the strings.

If it's all fake, the LEAST the people in charge can do is give me some juicier story lines to work with.

HOW ABOUT "GREG GETS A GIRLFRIEND"? OR "GREG GETS A MOTORCYCLE"? OR "GREG GETS A GIRLFRIEND AND A MOTORCYCLE"?

Every once in a while I wonder if the people in my life are who they SEEM to be, or if they're really just ACTORS.

If they're actors, I hope the kid who's playing my friend Rowley gets an award, because he's doing a great job pretending to be a doofus.

And if my brother Rodrick is actually just some guy getting PAID to act like a jerk, then that makes me see him in a whole new light.

Who knows? Maybe he's a nice guy in real life, and one day we'll be good friends.

But if my PARENTS are actors, then that's just wrong.

I've made a lot of Mother's and Father's Day cards over the years. If this is all a sham, then I deserve to get paid for my time and effort.

And speaking of getting paid, I'll bet my REAL parents are set for life, thanks to me.

But I'm doing everything I can to make sure I can cash in later. On most TV shows, the main character has a catchphrase that they say at least once per episode. So I've come up with a catchphrase of my OWN, and I drop it into conversation every once in a while.

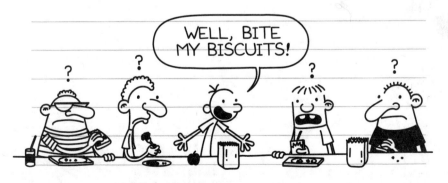

Later on I'm gonna slap my catchphrase on every piece of merchandise I can think of and wait for the money to start rolling in.

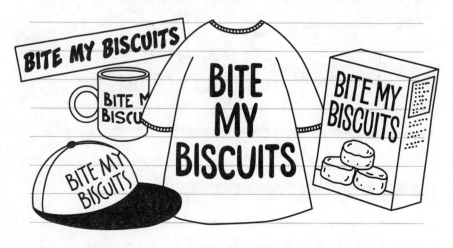

I'll guarantee THIS, though. I'm not gonna end up as one of those washed-up celebrities who sells pictures at autograph conventions just to make a cheap buck.

The one thing I've learned about television is that sooner or later, every show gets canceled. But in the last season they usually introduce a new pet or a cute kid to bump up the ratings.

So when my little brother, Manny, was born, I figured they were trying to replace me as the star of the show with a fresh new face.

I KNOW EXACTLY WHAT THIS IS!

The thing I couldn't figure out was how a newborn baby could be an ACTOR. I thought maybe Manny was a puppet being controlled by an adult who was hidden from view.

I never found any evidence that this was true, but that didn't stop me from checking every once in a while just to make sure.

As Manny got older, it was pretty clear he was getting around on his own. So then I wondered if he was actually a super-high-tech windup toy or even some kind of ROBOT.

Then I thought maybe EVERYBODY around me was a robot and I was the only actual human being in the family. Robots need electricity for power, so that would explain why we have two or three outlets in every room of the house.

It would ALSO explain some of the things my parents say when they think I'm not listening.

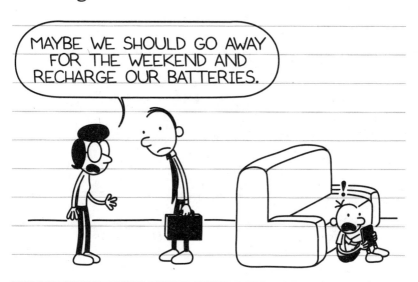

If robots use batteries, it explains why we have so many of them in the plastic bin in the laundry room. I'm not exactly sure where the batteries GO, but I do have a few guesses.

I figured the only way to find out if my family members were robots was to see if I could get one of them to short-circuit. But either Dad's a waterproof model or he's just a regular human with no sense of humor.

THAT incident got me grounded for a week. The people watching my show probably had a good laugh, but I'm sure the ratings were in the toilet for a while after that.

I guess there's a chance that I'm just an ordinary kid living a normal life, and I'm NOT the star of some TV show. But there could still be SOMEONE out there watching.

With all the planets in the universe, there's GOTTA be intelligent life out there. Some people say that if aliens were real, UFOs would be zipping around our skies all the time. But I figure aliens are SMART, and they're just keeping a low profile until the time is right to invade.

They're probably spying on us at this very second, gathering information about the way we live our lives.

My bet is that houseflies are actually little drones that the aliens use to beam images back to their ships. Because if you've ever seen a picture of a fly up close, it's pretty obvious their "eyes" are actually high-tech cameras.

The only thing I don't understand is that aliens seem to be really fascinated with dog poop. But I guess they've got their reasons for that.

I've tried to explain my theories to my parents and other grown-ups, but it's pretty clear nobody wants to hear what some kid has to say. So every chance I get, I make sure the aliens know I'm on their side.

I hope I got it right about the flies, though. Because if the drones are actually MOSQUITOES, we can probably expect an alien invasion any second now.

The thing is, I've ALWAYS felt like someone's out there keeping tabs on my life.

After my grandmother passed away, Mom told me I'd be safe because Nana was watching over me from heaven. I think that's great and all, but I've got a lot of issues with the way it works.

I'm fine with Nana watching over me when I'm riding a skateboard or doing something where I could use a little extra protection. But there are other times when you just need some privacy.

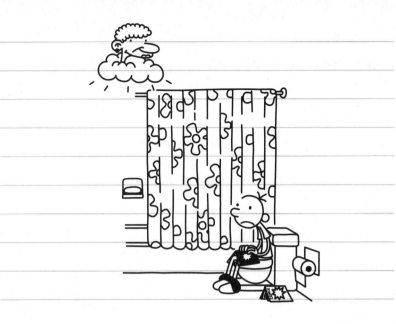

What worries me is that, when Nana was alive, sometimes I could be pretty obnoxious. So if I was her, I wouldn't really CARE if something happened to me.

If Nana looks the other way when I'm crossing the street or something like that, I can't say I blame her.

I actually feel kind of BAD if Nana has to keep an eye on me twenty-four hours a day. She worked hard all her life as a waitress, so she earned the right to RELAX.

I hope she's sitting in a bubble bath up there in heaven reading her romance novels, and not watching some ungrateful middle school kid doing his homework every night.

I'll tell you THIS: If I get into heaven, I'm gonna spend all my time swimming in a giant pool filled with jelly beans or doing loop-the-loops around the clouds.

YAHOOO!

There's no chance I'm gonna get stuck watching over some great grandkid I hardly even knew.

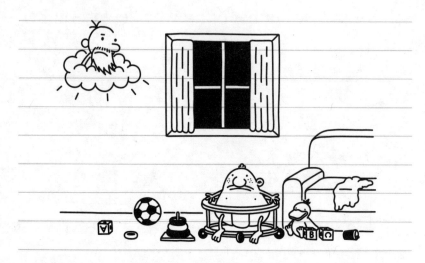

The only thing that will make it fun is if I have the power to punish my descendants whenever they do something annoying.

Recently, Mom told me it's not just NANA who's watching over me, it's ALL my relatives who've passed away.

I kind of wish she hadn't told me that, because now when I copy off of Alex Aruda's paper during a spelling test, I feel a lot more guilty about it.

I want to know how many generations this thing goes BACK. I'm fine with a few hundred years or so, but if it's my whole family tree all the way to the beginning, that's a totally different story.

I mean, if I've got relatives from caveman times watching over me, those guys are probably gonna be pretty confused by what I do on an average day.

To be honest, I'm not comfortable with all these people looking over my shoulder. If my relatives are really watching me every time I step out of the shower or taste my earwax, it's gonna be pretty awkward when we reunite later on.

Thursday

We have the book fair at school this week, and this morning Mom gave me twenty dollars to spend.

I THOUGHT I was allowed to pick whatever I wanted, but it turns out Mom expected me to spend the money on BOOKS.

When you get the chance to own a giant pencil with googly eyes, though, it's kind of hard to pass up.

SCRIBBLE
SCRIBBLE

Besides the pencil, I got a poster with a cat saying something sarcastic, an eraser shaped like a panda, a calculator that glows in the dark, a pen that writes underwater, and another giant pencil with googly eyes, just in case the first one gets lost or stolen.

I thought there was a chance Mom might not be happy with the way I spent her money, so I made sure to also buy a yo-yo with a good message on it.

But Mom wasn't impressed. She says I have to go back tomorrow and trade in all the stuff I bought for books.

Mom says the brain is like a muscle, and if you don't exercise it by reading and doing creative stuff, it'll get weak and mushy.

She says video games and TV are making my brain flabby, and if something doesn't change I'm basically gonna be a mindless zombie for the rest of my life.

Mom said if I turned off the television and put down my game controller, I might discover a talent I never knew I had.

That's a nice idea and all, but I feel like every time Mom's tried to get me to step out of my comfort zone, I've fallen flat on my face.

In the third grade we had a Poetry unit in school, and when I showed her what I was working on, Mom was pretty impressed. She sent one of my poems off to the National Poetry Council to see if THEY thought it was any good.

Two weeks later, we got a letter back in the mail.

NATIONAL POETRY COUNCIL

Dear Gregory Heffley,

Congratulations! Your poem, "My Silly Summer," has been chosen to appear in the prestigious *Poetry Anthology,* an annual collection of the nation's best work by the most promising poets.

Mom was REALLY excited about the news, and I admit I was, too. I kind of got into the idea of being a poet, and even started to dress differently at school.

But it turns out the whole "Poetry Anthology" thing was a big JOKE. First of all, the book was about a thousand pages long, and all the poems were in really tiny print. It took me a half hour to find my poem in there, and they spelled my name wrong, anyway.

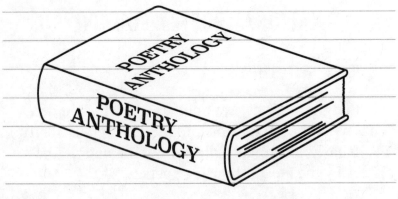

I read a few of the other poems, and they were AWFUL. Most of them seemed like they were written by five-year-olds.

My Turtle Fred
by Maya Peebles

My turtle Fred
He is not dead
He sleeps in his shell
And when he does die
I guess he will smell

It was pretty obvious that ANYONE could have their poem included in this book, and the whole "nation's best work" thing was just a bunch of baloney. I guess the way the National Poetry Council makes money is by selling the book to all the suckers who got PUBLISHED in it.

What I know for sure is, the Poetry Council made a LOT of money off of us. Mom bought ten copies to hand out to relatives, and the books were eighty bucks a pop.

Plus, she bought a few extra copies for ME, in case I wanted to give them to my kids one day.

The National Poetry Council kept sending us letters and calling, asking us to buy more books, and I think after a while Mom finally realized it was all just a giant scam.

My copies of the "Poetry Anthology" are in the laundry room, but at least they're being put to good use.

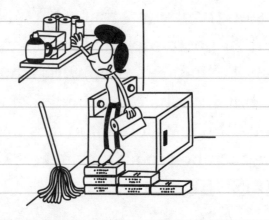

Once Mom got it in her head that I was SPECIAL, she wouldn't let it go. She even tried to get me into the Talented and Gifted program at school.

In my elementary school, all the really smart kids were in the Talented and Gifted program.

But I guess the teachers didn't want us regular kids to feel bad about ourselves, so when they called the Talented and Gifted group out of class for their meetings, they used a code name.

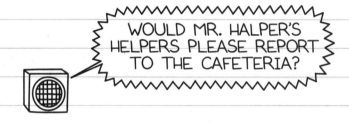

WOULD MR. HALPER'S HELPERS PLEASE REPORT TO THE CAFETERIA?

Mr. Halper was our janitor, and for a long time I thought the kids in Mr. Halper's Helpers were just volunteers who wanted to give him a hand emptying the trash and stuff like that.

Then I finally realized that Mr. Halper's Helpers were all the brainiest kids in our grade.

Mom thought I belonged in Talented and Gifted, so she tried to convince the school to let me in. But I had to take a TEST to prove I was smart enough.

I don't remember everything on the test, but I do remember one of the questions.

Fill in the blank:

Johnny is the best at math.
Johnny is the best at swimming.
Johnny is the best at reading.
Johnny is _____.

Looking back, I guess I was supposed to write down something else Johnny was the best at. But I really didn't like this Johnny character, so I wrote something different.

Johnny is __a show-off__.

Even though I totally flunked the test, Mom was mad at the school because she thought I was smart enough to be in Talented and Gifted. But believe me, those kids are on a whole different level.

I'm actually kind of grateful I didn't make the cut, because in middle school, kids like Alex Aruda have to stay inside during recess to do the teachers' tax returns.

I guess Mom felt pretty bad I didn't get into Talented and Gifted, but a few weeks later she told me some good news. She said I got picked by the school to be in a special club called the "Champs" that had secret meetings twice a week.

Well, I was really excited about this Champs thing and was nervous when I went to my first secret meeting. But it turns out the Champs were just kids like me who had trouble pronouncing their "R"s, and we had to work with Mrs. Pressey on Tuesdays and Thursdays in the library to try to improve.

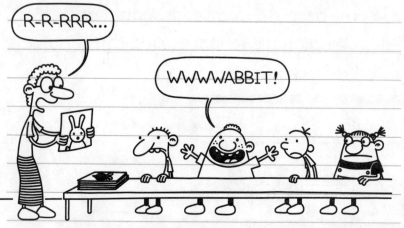

I don't know who came up with the Champs name, but let me tell you, we thought it was AWESOME.

During recess, if the Champs were coming through, all the other kids got out of the way.

The only kids who didn't like us were the Language Lizards, which was the group that met on Mondays and Wednesdays to work on their "S" sounds. But I think the Language Lizards were just jealous of us because they had such a lousy name.

KICK

Me and the other Champs were tight, and I really looked forward to those Tuesday and Thursday meetings because they always ended up turning into a free-for-all.

But Mom got frustrated that I wasn't making any progress with my Rs, so she hired a private tutor to work with me after school. And after a few months, I could say my Rs with no problem.

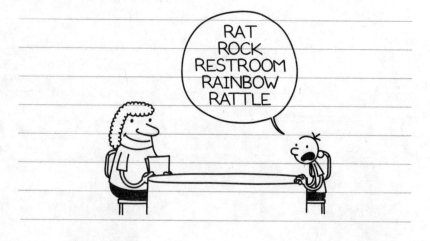

Unfortunately, that meant I didn't need to be in the Champs anymore. For a few weeks I actually FAKED like I couldn't say my Rs just so I could stay in the club. But one day I let my guard down and slipped up.

From that day on I was an outcast. Even the Language Lizards didn't want anything to do with me.

I guess EVERY parent thinks their kid is special, even when they're not. But I think it's starting to get a little out of control.

Manny played soccer this spring, and his team STUNK. They never got a single goal, and the other teams scored at least ten times a game. It didn't help that their goalie, Tucker Remy, spent the whole time stuffing grass in his belly button.

At the end of the season, they had a trophy ceremony. I thought only the kids on the WINNING team would get trophies, which is how it worked back when I played soccer. But I guess some parents were worried the kids on the losing teams might feel bad about themselves, so this year EVERYONE got a trophy.

They were GOOD trophies, too. They were gigantic and made of metal, not cheap plastic like the ones handed out when I was little. And no kid was more proud to get his trophy than Tucker Remy.

I wonder if these kids will be messed up later on in life, though. Because I know those soccer trophies are having an effect on ME. Every so often I'll think about entering a contest at school, but when I see the size of the trophies, I lose interest.

Friday

Today I returned most of the stuff I bought from the book fair, but when Mom saw what I got to replace it, she wasn't all that thrilled.

I traded for a bunch of those Spineticklers books everyone at school is so crazy about.

Mom said she wanted me to get books that were more "challenging," but I didn't really have much of a choice. Since the book fair is a few weeks before Halloween, this is the kind of stuff they're selling.

44

I'd say about 90% of the books at the fair were from the Spineticklers series. There were a bunch of Spineticklers rip-offs, too. I don't know if it's legal to do that kind of thing, but something about it doesn't seem right.

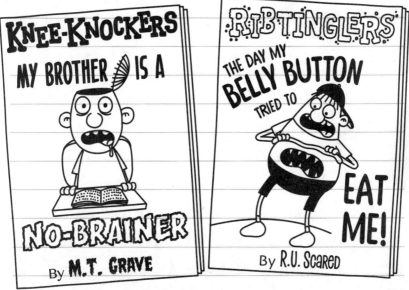

KNEE-KNOCKERS
MY BROTHER IS A
NO-BRAINER
By M.T. GRAVE

RIBTINGLERS
THE DAY MY BELLY BUTTON TRIED TO
EAT ME!
By R.U. SCARED

It feels like these scary books just came out of NOWHERE. The last series that was really popular at my school was the Underpants Bandits books, but those are yesterday's news now.

In fact, I saw a kid walking down the hall with an Underpants Bandits book earlier this week, and an eighth-grader gave him an atomic wedgie.

I'm not usually a big fan of scary stories, because when I read them I end up having nightmares.

But Rowley's even more of a chicken than I am, because all the books HE picked out were from the Spineticklers JUNIOR series, which are supposed to be for kindergartners.

At least I'm brave enough for the REAL
stuff. One of the books I bought is about this
guy who gets frozen and then wakes up in
the future.

I thought it was just a bunch of science
fiction, but Albert Sandy said he heard about
this rich guy who's doing it for REAL.

Albert said he saw this news report about an old billionaire who's really sick, and he paid a ton of money to freeze himself. Then, in a hundred years, he's gonna get UNfrozen. He's betting that by then they'll know how to cure every disease and he can go on living forever.

This freezing thing sounds like a great plan to ME. And if I strike it rich one day, I'm gonna do the EXACT same thing.

But I'm not gonna wait till I'm old like that billionaire.

The way I see it, if you freeze yourself when you're too old, then when they unfreeze you in the future, you're gonna be too grumpy to have any fun.

So if I win the lottery or something in the next few years, I'm gonna use the money to buy myself a one-way ticket to the future.

I'm not telling anyone about my plan, though. There's this jerk at our school named Phillip Crivello, and his parents are rich.

So if he gets the same idea as me, I could still be dealing with him a hundred years from now.

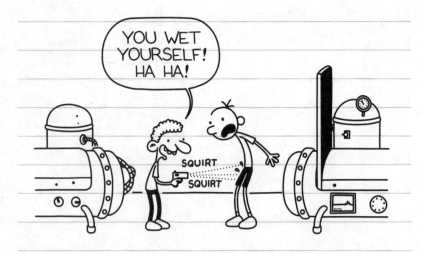

But I'm not sure if a hundred years is far enough to go.

By then I'm sure I'll have a bunch of great nieces and nephews who need babysitting, and I'm not spending all that money just so I can change a bunch of dirty diapers in the future.

I'm planning on staying frozen a lot longer, like a THOUSAND years, because by then things will be REALLY interesting.

I'm not willing to go any further than that, though, because who KNOWS how much human beings will have evolved by then.

If I DON'T win the lottery in the next few years, I guess I'm gonna have to find a cheaper option. Albert Sandy said that people who can't afford to get their whole body frozen can just freeze their BRAINS.

I'm kind of nervous handing my brain off to some people I don't even know, though. I'm guessing they're not paying their employees a lot of money to basically wait around and do nothing, so I'm kind of concerned about the quality of help they have working at these freezing places.

After your brain gets unfrozen, I guess they'll put it in a robot body, which probably takes a lot of getting used to.

But if I can scrape together enough money, I'm gonna freeze my WHOLE body and do it RIGHT. Because whenever you go with the cheaper option, you end up regretting it.

<u>Saturday</u>

There are only a few weeks to go until Halloween, and my family spent the morning putting up our decorations in front of the house.

We used to keep it really basic and hung some cobwebs, a few jack-o'-lanterns, and a plastic spider or two. But then our neighbors started going all out on Halloween, and suddenly our decorations looked pretty skimpy.

So last year Mom handed Rodrick forty bucks and told him to go out and pick up some more stuff for the front porch.

But Rodrick blew it all on this really awful
electronic plastic witch.

The way it works is, if you clap or make a
loud noise, the witch lets out this
bloodcurdling cackle that goes on
FOREVER. Then it shakes and its eyes
glow red.

But whoever created that thing set the volume too high, and there's no way to turn it down. You have to wait for the witch to go through its whole routine, which is like two minutes long.

We hung it out over the front porch last year, but little kids were too scared of the thing, and the only trick-or-treaters we had were the teenagers who came by after 10 p.m.

The day after Halloween, Dad put the witch on a shelf in the furnace room in the basement, and that's where it's been ever since. But that doesn't mean it's stopped causing PROBLEMS.

The witch is SUPER sensitive to sound, and sometimes the slightest noise will set it off, even if the noise is on a different floor.

To make matters WORSE, the witch seems to have a mind of its own, and sometimes it'll go off randomly even if no one makes a PEEP. I've had at least two sleepovers end early because of that thing.

I've been trying all year to convince Mom and Dad to throw the witch away, but Dad says it's just a plastic toy and I need to stop being such a scaredy-cat.

But I guess Mom got sick of the witch randomly going off all the time, and a few weeks ago she told Dad to go downstairs and take the batteries out, which he did.

And what happened NEXT is the reason I haven't been in the furnace room ever since.

What stinks is that all my old Halloween costumes are down in the furnace room. So unless Mom's willing to spring for something NEW, I guess I'm not going trick-or-treating this year.

<u>Sunday</u>

Well, all the hard work we put into decorating for Halloween yesterday got wiped out.

A bunch of geese got at the jack-o'-lanterns in the middle of the night and made a HUGE mess.

Every fall, geese flying south for the winter make a pit stop in our town and stick around for a few weeks before heading back out. Usually they poop all over the soccer field at the town park, but other than that they're pretty harmless.

For some reason, though, this year they're SUPER aggressive toward people.

For the past few weeks, me and Rowley have been getting ambushed just about every day on our walk home from school.

And the geese aren't just going after KIDS, either. Whenever Dad goes out to get the mail, he's gotta arm himself for battle.

Dad wants to call Animal Control to clear the geese off our street, but Mom won't let him.

She says geese have been flocking to these parts for thousands of years, and if anything, WE'RE the ones intruding on THEIR lives.

I'm personally fine with animals, as long as they keep their distance. But I think if we don't draw a line somewhere, we're just headed for trouble.

My science teacher said that 40,000 years ago, dogs used to be wild animals, just like wolves. But then I guess they saw our warm fires and cozy caves and wanted to get in on the action. So they wagged their tails and did a few tricks and that's all it took.

61

Nowadays, dogs have it MADE. People spend all kinds of money buying them gourmet food and cushiony beds.

I'm sure the reason wolves seem so ticked off all the time is because they're just jealous THEY didn't think of kissing up to people first.

CATS aren't stupid either. Last summer Mrs. Fredericks up the street fed a stray cat that was hanging out in her yard, and each night after that MORE cats came. Now the cats have completely taken over her house, and she recently had to sell her car so she could afford to keep feeding them.

We've got problems with our OWN pet,
which is a PIG. Personally, I think it should
live outside in a pen or a shed or something,
but instead it lives inside the house with
US. And not only does it use the same
bathtub as me, but I'm 99% sure it's been
using my TOOTHBRUSH, too.

And that thing is SMART, which makes me
kind of nervous.

In fact, I think it's been trying to learn how to COMMUNICATE with us. Manny has this toy called a "See-and-Talk," where you pull a string and it says a word.

Somehow, the pig figured out how to USE the See-and-Talk, and every so often it manages to put together a full sentence.

Lately I've been thinking there's gotta be a way the two of us can team up. I've heard a pig's sense of smell is 2,000 times better than a human being's. That talent could really come in handy.

Mom always buys the Halloween candy for trick-or-treaters a few weeks early, and she hides it somewhere so the rest of us don't get at it. I've turned the house upside down looking for it, but so far no luck. And if the pig knows what I'm looking for, it's not being very helpful.

This time of year is TORTURE for a kid. There are all these candy commercials on TV, and every time you walk into the grocery store it's like they're TRYING to mess with you.

But Mom says I can't have any candy until Halloween night, which I think is totally cruel.

I think I've figured out a way to get my hands on some candy BEFORE Halloween, though. My school is having a contest called the "Balloon Brigade," which it does every October.

Each student gets a helium balloon, and everyone releases theirs at the same time. They give you these little cards to write your name and address on, and when people find the balloons they're supposed to send them back.

GREETINGS FROM THE **BALLOON BRIGADE!**

PLEASE SEND THIS BALLOON BACK TO THE ADDRESS WRITTEN ON THE REVERSE SIDE OF THIS CARD AND LET US KNOW HOW FAR IT TRAVELED!

The school has a big map on a bulletin board near the library, and when a kid turns in a balloon, Vice Principal Roy uses a thumbtack to mark how far it went.

At the end of the week he measures the distance each balloon traveled to find out whose went the farthest, and that kid gets a REWARD.

Last year, Andrea Gennarro's balloon traveled forty-three miles, and she won a thirty-dollar gift certificate for the book fair.

But THIS year the grand prize is a giant jar of candy corn, which is sitting in Vice Principal Roy's office right now.

The school puts a little code on each balloon so nobody cheats and turns in a store-bought balloon.

I've never had one of my balloons sent back to me, though. I need to make SURE that whoever finds mine doesn't just ignore me, so I wrote a three-page letter that I'm hoping will get a response.

68

Because when it comes to free candy, I'm not messing around.

> To whoever finds this balloon:
>
> I am a lonely child without any friends. I released this balloon hoping it would find its way to a kind person who might write me back and bring some joy to my life.

Monday

After lunch today the teachers led us all out to the basketball court for the big Balloon Brigade launch. I still get kind of nervous stepping foot on the blacktop, because that's where the Cheese sat for a year and a half. There's even a stain where it used to be.

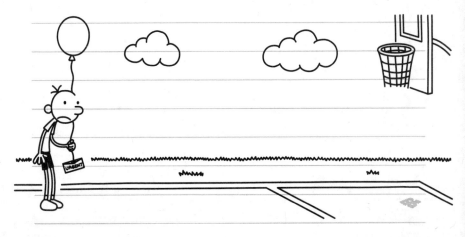

It's been a long time since the Cheese terrorized our school, but I guess some people actually LIKED having something to be scared of. A few different times kids have tried to start the Cheese Touch back up, but the teachers are on the lookout because they don't want to have to go through all that nonsense again.

One kid actually managed to sneak a piece of lunch meat onto the court during recess, but the Roast Beef Touch didn't have the same ring to it.

Still, someone's ALWAYS trying to start some new thing. This year it's all about the chairs in the auditorium.

The chairs are red except ONE, which is yellow and has a busted leg. Apparently some kid peed on it during a really long assembly last month. And if you're not paying attention and sit in the yellow chair, you're pretty much finished for the rest of the school year.

If you ask me, people should just be happy the Cheese Touch is behind us and stop trying to replace it with something else. Because the last thing you need in middle school is anything EXTRA to worry about.

Today, Vice Principal Roy did a countdown on his bullhorn and everyone released their balloons. I have to admit, it was kind of exciting to see all of them go up in the air at the same time.

But the excitement didn't last LONG.

Almost all of the balloons went straight into the new cell phone tower they built on the hill next to the football field, and didn't go any farther.

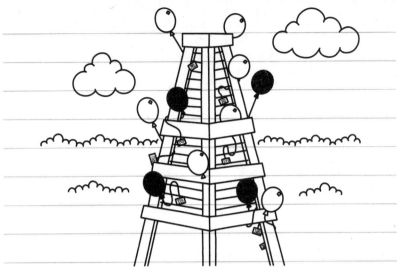

Luckily, my balloon was weighed down by the letter I wrote, so it went UNDER the tower, and then it cleared the trees on the other side.

I don't think my balloon is gonna make it as far as Andrea Gennarro's did, but I don't NEED it to. As long as someone finds the balloon and sends it back, that jar of candy corn is MINE.

I just hope they write instead of call. I put Mom's cell phone number on my letter, but apparently it's gonna be a few days before they fix the tower and people in town can get service again.

<u>Wednesday</u>

It's been two days, and still no word on my balloon. I'm starting to get a little worried, because the contest ends Monday, and if nobody gets their balloon back, I'm sure Vice Principal Roy is gonna keep the candy for HIMSELF.

Lately I've been having trouble staying focused at school, but luckily my homework hasn't been that hard. Our reading assignment was to write a biography on a famous author, so I chose the Spineticklers guy.

But it turns out there's barely ANY information on him. In fact, the only thing I could find was the little blurb in the back of his books.

Who is I.M. SPOOKY?

Almost nothing is known about the mysterious I.M. Spooky. All we can say for sure is that he's cooking up a terrifying new entry in the Spineticklers series!

The good news is that since I wasn't really able to find anything on I.M. Spooky, I was finished with my entire author's bio in about two minutes.

```
┌─────────────────────────────────────────┐
│          AUTHOR BIOGRAPHY               │
│                                         │
│  AUTHOR NAME: I.M. Spooky               │
│                                         │
│  BIRTHDATE: ???                         │
│                                         │
│  PLACE OF BIRTH: ???                    │
│                                         │
│  HOBBIES: ???                           │
│                                         │
│  EDUCATION: ???                         │
│                                         │
│  INTERESTING FACTS ABOUT                │
│  THE AUTHOR:                            │
│            ???                          │
└─────────────────────────────────────────┘
```

With a name like I.M. Spooky, I guess you have no CHOICE but to write scary books for a living.

I kind of wish I had never started reading those Spineticklers books, though. Because once you start reading them, it's hard to STOP. And they're starting to affect my everyday life.

Going to the dentist was never that much fun to begin with, but after I read Spineticklers number 67, it got even WORSE.

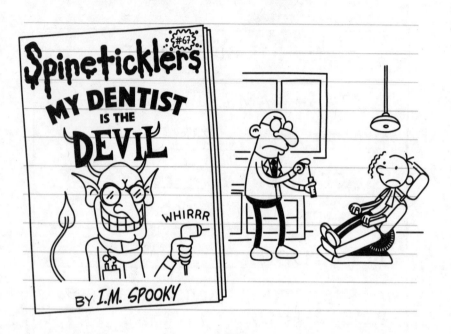

I've checked out every Spineticklers book from the library, and I even borrowed a few Spineticklers Junior books from Rowley so I could keep going.

And just like I predicted, the books are starting to give me nightmares. Spineticklers number 71 is about this kid who grows a lizard tail and tries to hide it from his family and teachers.

That one really stressed me out, and the night I read it, I had a dream that I was the one with the tail.

Actually, my dream started off really GOOD, because there are a bunch of fun things you can do with a tail that you wouldn't even think of.

In my dream I wasn't ashamed of my tail, I was PROUD of it. And I used it to its full advantage.

The only thing I didn't like about it was that when I got excited about something, everyone could tell.

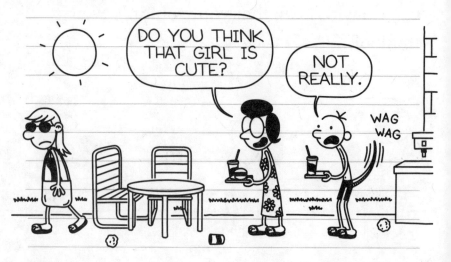

Then all of a sudden my tail became a
PROBLEM. People got jealous, and the
next thing I knew, I was being hunted like I
was some kind of monster.

I ran for my LIFE and escaped through a
window, and the townspeople chased me
down the street and through a shopping
mall. I almost got away, but then my tail
got stuck in the escalator.

I swear I could actually FEEL it happen, and it woke me up.

In fact, the dream was so realistic that I turned on the light to see if I actually DID have a tail. And I have to say, I was a little disappointed when I realized that nothing was there.

That's not the ONLY bad dream I've had because of those books, though.

80

The other night I had a dream where I was captured by zombie pirates and made to walk the plank. For some reason, I kept repeating this stupid rhyme.

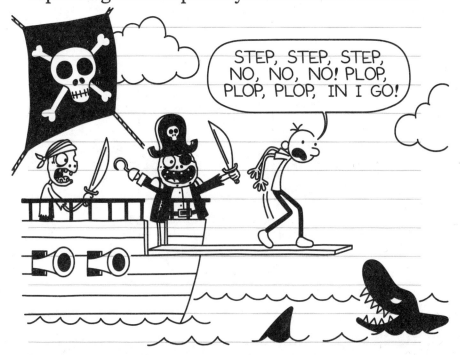

Unfortunately, I was saying it for REAL, so now Rodrick has a video of me talking in my sleep.

Sometimes my dreams are so ridiculous I actually KNOW I'm having a nightmare. And when that happens, I try to snap out of it.

Other times I THINK I'm having a nightmare but I'm actually NOT. Then when I try to wake myself up, I realize I'm not asleep.

Mom has this book that explains how to make sense of dreams, and it's actually pretty interesting. Basically everything that happens in your dreams has some kind of deeper meaning.

Falling

A dream about falling means you have a fear of losing control of your life. It could also mean you're afraid you don't have enough time to get everything done.

Apparently the one about the tail means I'm ashamed of something in my past. And the dream about the pirates means I'm stressed out about not being a good enough friend.

The other night I had a dream that all my teeth were loose, and apparently that one's about a fear of getting older, which kind of makes sense.

But it's gonna take me FOREVER to decode the dream I had LAST night, because that one was just completely bonkers.

Thursday

It turns out picking the Spineticklers author for my reading assignment was a bad call. Almost ALL the kids in my class did their author biographies on I.M. Spooky, and NOBODY could find any information on the guy. I think our teacher, Mrs. Mott, thought we were trying to be funny, so she said we all had to stay in for recess every day until we redid our assignment.

84

I think part of why Mrs. Mott got so mad is
that she's getting sick of everyone doing
their book reports on the Spineticklers
series.

Last week at least five kids picked the exact
same book for their assignment, and it just
about pushed Mrs. Mott over the edge.

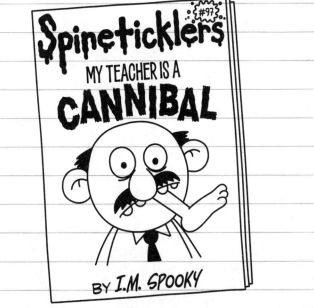

But the last straw was when Amanda Pickler did a Book Talk on "The Brain with a Mind of Its Own." Amanda brought in a fake brain made out of Jell-O, but she lost her grip and dropped it on the floor, which made two kids pass out.

A bunch of parents aren't happy about the Spineticklers books, either. I heard that Danny McGlurk's dad went to last week's PTA meeting and said he wanted the books banned because they promote WITCHCRAFT.

Apparently, Mr. McGlurk caught Danny dabbling in the "dark arts" in his garage, and Mr. McGlurk blamed it all on the Spineticklers books.

But the way I heard it, Danny was just practicing magic tricks for the fall talent show.

I seriously hope the Spineticklers books don't get banned, because they're the only thing keeping my reading grade up.

We're required to read fifteen books by the end of the year, and ALL of mine are from that series. The way you prove you finished reading a book is by taking a multiple-choice test on the computer.

I've gotten a 100% on every single test I've taken so far, which I guess proves I'm really paying attention when I read the books.

QUESTION 12:

Who did the Chattering Chompers eat?

○ Mother   ○ Baby Ellis
○ Father   ● All of the above

When I got home, I told Mom how Mrs. Mott was making us redo our author biographies, and I didn't know what to do.

But Mom told me the reason I couldn't find any information on I.M. Spooky is because he's not an actual PERSON.

I told Mom that was ridiculous because this guy has written almost 200 books. But Mom said sometimes publishers create a fictional author and then hire a bunch of people to write books under that name.

I gotta say, if that's true I feel kind of cheated. But I feel worse for ROWLEY, because he wasted his time writing I.M. Spooky a letter.

Dear Mr. Spooky,
First of all let me say I am a huge fan. But the reason I am writing is to complain that the book "Scaredy Cat and the Haunted House" was WAY too scary.

Mom was trying to help me find a different author who's an actual human being when there was a knock at our door. I answered it, and there was a lady and some kid I'd never seen before.

I was pretty spooked when she asked if my name was Greg Heffley. That's when I saw the deflated balloon in the kid's hand, and I put two and two together.

At first I was kind of excited, because if someone found my BALLOON, that meant I was gonna get that giant jar of candy corn. But then I remembered what I wrote in my letter and wished I could take some of it back.

And finally, if you find this balloon and return it to me without delay, I can promise you a large cash reward. I have a rich uncle and I'm sure he'd be happy to hook you up.

Sincerely, *Greg Heffley*

I didn't want these people thinking I was some weird kid who makes friends by sending out letters attached to helium balloons. But I guess it didn't really matter. I figured I could just take my balloon back and send them on their way.

Before I knew it, though, Mom was at the front door, and she invited them INSIDE. Thirty seconds later we had these two total strangers sitting at our kitchen table.

The lady introduced herself as Mrs. Selsam and said her son's name was Maddox. They live in the next town over. Apparently this kid Maddox was practicing the violin in his bedroom and saw the balloon dangling from a tree branch outside.

Mrs. Selsam said their house is way out in the sticks, and they don't really have any neighbors. Plus, because she works full-time and goes to school at night, she doesn't get many chances to set up "playdates" for Maddox.

She said that when she read the letter she knew it was "meant to be," and they got in the car and drove right over.

I was starting to get REALLY uncomfortable. All I was trying to do was win some candy corn, and now things were getting totally out of control.

But before I could explain this was all a big misunderstanding, Mom told me I should take Maddox upstairs and get to know him while she chatted with Mrs. Selsam in the kitchen.

So now this kid was in my ROOM. And it seemed like it was just as awkward for HIM as it was for ME.

I tried making conversation, but I couldn't get a WORD out of him. Eventually I gave up and just pretended he wasn't there.

When I turned on my computer to play a video game, though, Maddox turned into a TOTALLY different person. He got all worked up and started making strange noises.

I didn't know WHAT was going on, but five seconds later Mrs. Selsam came running into my room and turned off my monitor. She said she doesn't allow Maddox to play video games, and the reason he was so "animated" was because he'd never actually SEEN one before.

I wish she hadn't said her kid doesn't play video games, because I didn't need Mom getting any crazy ideas.

Maddox was having trouble calming down, so Mrs. Selsam said they should probably be heading home. And that was just fine by ME. But I wish I hadn't been so eager to get them out the door, because after they drove away I realized I never did get my balloon back.

<u>Saturday</u>

Yesterday I told Vice Principal Roy that someone found my balloon, but he wouldn't hand over the candy corn unless I brought the balloon in to prove it.

So today when Mom said she wanted to take me to Maddox's house for a get-together, I was all for it. I figured I'd make a little chitchat, grab the balloon, and be on my way.

But Mom had OTHER plans. When we got to the Selsams' house, which really WAS in the middle of nowhere, Mom said she was gonna go into town and have coffee with Mrs. Selsam while I hung back with Maddox.

Believe me, if I would've known THAT was gonna be the deal, I never would've gotten in the car.

When Mom dropped me off, I figured I might as well try to make the most of it. Maddox was actually TALKING this time, so that was a decent start at least.

I asked Maddox if he had any junk food, but he said his mom doesn't let him have any of that kind of stuff. I asked him if he wanted to watch some TV, but he told me they didn't HAVE a television.

At first I thought he was joking, but sure enough, in the family room there was a BOOKSHELF where the TV was supposed to go.

In fact, there were books EVERYWHERE in this house.

I asked Maddox what he does for fun, and he said he either practices his violin or plays with his Legos. I was pretty relieved to hear that he actually had some TOYS, because I was starting to wonder about this kid.

But when he showed me what he had in his bedroom, I was totally blown away.

He had a whole Lego CITY in there. Maddox said he wants to be an engineer when he grows up, and whenever he asks for a Lego set, his mom buys it for him. All I can say is, she must have spent a FORTUNE.

I wanted to play with some of the big sets Maddox had, but he wouldn't let me go anywhere NEAR them.

He told me if I wanted to play with his Legos, I could use the pieces from his "leftovers" bin. That was a pretty big letdown, because the leftovers bin was filled with a bunch of random pieces.

So while Maddox was putting together a 500-piece Lego spaceship, I did the best with what I had.

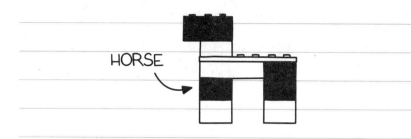

HORSE

After about an hour and a half, Mom and Mrs. Selsam finally came back. Luckily, my balloon was sitting on the little table next to the front door, so I grabbed it on the way out.

But just when I was about to get in the car, Mrs. Selsam came running out with Maddox right behind her. Maddox said I "stole" from him. I tried to explain that the balloon was actually MINE, and I was just taking it BACK.

But Maddox wasn't talking about the
BALLOON. He said I stole one of his
LEGOS. Apparently one of the pieces was
missing from his leftovers bin. And don't
even ask me how he knew THAT.

I swore up and down I didn't take any of
his Legos, and I even turned my pockets
inside out to prove it. But he STILL wasn't
satisfied.

So I actually let Maddox and Mrs. Selsam
pat me down, which was totally humiliating.
But I gotta admit it was pretty satisfying
when they couldn't find anything on me.

After that I thought I was in the clear, and I
turned to get in the car.

That's when Maddox spotted a Lego that was stuck to my elbow.

What really stinks is that it was one of those tiny square pieces, and I'm sure Maddox had a BILLION of those in his leftovers bin.

ACTUAL
SIZE

Anyway, that's how our "playdate" ended.

On a positive note, I got what I came for. But on the way home, Mom seemed pretty upset. I thought she was mad about the Lego piece, but she wasn't.

She said she was disappointed I didn't hit it off with Maddox, because she thought he was a good "role model" for me.

But if Mom wants to connect me with someone I'll actually look UP to, she's gonna have to try a little harder.

Monday

For the past few days, Mom's been doing an experiment on me and Rodrick. She wanted to see how long we'd go before one of us would take out the trash without being told. But I guess we failed the test, because last night she gave up.

At dinner, Mom said she didn't go to college just so she could spend her time cleaning up after everyone and scraping gum off our shoes. She said she needed to be in a "stimulating environment" and was going back to school full-time to finish her master's degree.

She said that for this to work, everyone's gonna have to pitch in extra around the house. So to make chores "fun," she created a "Grab Bag," which is a pillowcase filled with little slips of paper that have random jobs written down on them.

I'm pretty sure she got the idea from "Family Frolic" magazine.

Me and Rodrick are supposed to reach into the Grab Bag every day after school and do a chore.

Mom told us that if we do our chores, she'll let us dip into the Halloween candy a little early.

Well, that's proof it's SOMEWHERE in the house. But that's just gonna be BONUS candy for me, because today at school I traded in my balloon for that big jar of candy corn in Vice Principal Roy's office. And as soon as I got home, I hid it in the bottom drawer of my dresser so I didn't have to share it with anyone.

After that was taken care of, I reached into the Grab Bag and pulled out a slip of paper and got "Polish the Silverware," which has to be the worst chore in there.

Rodrick must have added his OWN items to the Grab Bag, because I found him asleep next to a slip of paper with his handwriting on it.

I decided to help myself to some candy corn as a reward for finishing my chore, but when I walked into my room, my bottom drawer was open and the jar was EMPTY.

It didn't take me long to find the culprit. I found the pig stumbling around the kitchen like it was drunk or something.

At first I was mad, because not only did the pig eat all my candy corn, but it somehow figured out how to unscrew the jar to do it.

Then I started getting kind of WORRIED, because the pig really didn't look so good.

I figured Grandpa might know what to do, but he was out on a date with Mrs. Fredericks. I woke Rodrick up and asked HIM what to do, and he said I should call Dad. So I did, but Dad was in a meeting.

I didn't want to bother Mom, because I knew she was at her college signing up for classes. But the pig was turning green, so I called her anyway. I told her that the pig seemed pretty sick, and she asked me if it had eaten anything strange.

I really didn't wanna tell her it had gotten into my candy corn, so I told her I wasn't sure. She said we'd better take the pig to the vet just in case, and that she was leaving school and would meet us there.

Rodrick wasn't happy I was waking him up for the second time in five minutes, but one look at the pig convinced him we needed to get moving.

On the ride over, I held the pig in my arms in the back of Rodrick's van. But halfway to the vet the pig started making weird sounds.

I told Rodrick to pull over, but by the time he did it was already too late.

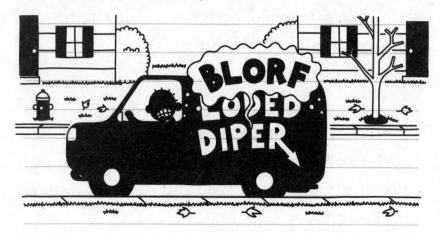

Now there was a giant, gooey, orange-and-yellow puddle on the floor of Rodrick's van. And I'm pretty sure I'll never be able to look at candy corn the same way again.

Rodrick said it was my fault for making the pig sick, so it was MY job to clean it up. Then he handed me a roll of paper towels and told me to get to work.

Even though the puddle was candy corn, it didn't SMELL like it. I tried mopping it up while holding my breath, but it was hopeless.

Finally I couldn't take it anymore and realized I was gonna get sick MYSELF. Fortunately, I was able to get out of the van in time.

UNFORTUNATELY, the lady whose yard we were parked in front of was outside raking leaves and saw the whole thing.

I guess she thought we were a couple of bad kids and this was some kind of juvenile prank, because she said she was calling the COPS.

So I got back in the van and we peeled out of there as fast as we could and turned on to the highway. But we didn't get far.

Luckily, I was able to explain everything to the police officer, but he didn't seem to want to hear all the details.

Just after the cop drove away, Mom spotted Rodrick's van on the highway and pulled in behind us. And I guess the pig hadn't totally emptied out yet, because it coughed up one last puddle of candy corn.

Tuesday
Last night when we got home, Mom said she wasn't mad at me, she was DISAPPOINTED. And when it comes to Mom, that's even WORSE.

She said she's disturbed by my "pattern of deception," and that between the incident at Maddox's house and what happened with the pig, she didn't feel like I could be trusted. I explained for the millionth time that the Lego thing was just a misunderstanding, but she'd obviously already made up her mind about that one.

The last time we had a conversation like this was when I was in the fourth grade, and I'll admit I totally deserved a punishment that time around.

It actually started with something kind of small. Mom used to pack my lunch every morning, and I'd always eat my sandwich and snack but toss whatever fruit she'd put in there.

Mom figured out I wasn't eating my fruit, so one day she put an apple in my lunch and made me promise to bring the core home to prove I'd eaten it. She said if I DIDN'T, she wouldn't pack a snack for me anymore.

At lunch I forgot all about my promise, and I threw my fruit away like usual.

112

And when I got home, Mom asked me
where my apple core was.

I probably should've just come clean, but
for some reason I made up a lie. I told her
that on the way to school that morning, a
bully grabbed me and stole my apple.

It was a pretty desperate move on my part,
but I was worried Mom wasn't gonna give
me a snack the next day if I told her the
truth.

I thought my story was so lame that Mom would see right through it. But she wanted to know more about this bully, so I really let it rip.

I told her the kid's name was Curtis Litz and that he was a foot taller than me, with a unibrow, and a mole on his chin. I figured if Mom was looking for DETAILS, I wasn't gonna disappoint her.

Mom said she could step in, but this was a good opportunity for me to learn how to settle a conflict on my OWN.

So that night she brought me a pen and paper and had me write Curtis a letter, which I did.

Dear Curtis,

Please don't take my apple again. My mom says I need it for my nutrition.

Sincerely,
Greg Heffley

I probably should've just ended it right then. But I wrote a fake letter to myself from Curtis instead. And to make sure Mom could see how BAD this kid was, I added a rude drawing at the end.

DEAR GREGORY,

YOUR APPLE WAS DELICIOUS. TELL YOUR MOMMY TO SEND ME ANOTHER ONE TOMORROW.

FROM CURTIS

A BUTT

Well, I guess I took it too far, because the next day Mom came to school with that letter, demanding to speak to Curtis Litz.

The secretary told Mom there was no student named Curtis Litz at the school, and when Mom asked me about him I said he must be homeschooled.

After that I got kind of nervous, and for the next two weeks I had Rowley eat my apple at lunch and give me the core.

Mom seemed to forget all about it until we sat a row behind the Bartlemans at church one weekend. Their fifth-grade son, Tevin, looked just like my description of Curtis Litz, and he caught Mom's eye.

Mom told Tevin's parents they're raising a rotten kid and that they owed her some apples. I felt pretty bad, because Tevin Bartleman is a nice kid and his family volunteers at the soup kitchen downtown every Saturday morning.

Later on in the year Mom joined the Fundraising Committee, which was headed up by Mrs. Bartleman. It didn't take long for Mom to figure things out from there, and I lost TV privileges for a whole month as punishment.

But I actually ended up getting a DOUBLE punishment, because for the rest of that year, every time Tevin saw me in the hallway, he really let me have it.

Last night Mom decided that my punishment for lying was for me to take THREE chores out of the Grab Bag every day this week.

Unfortunately, she already cleared out all of Rodrick's slips of paper, which means there's no chance I'll get an easy one.

When we wrapped up our conversation last night, Mom said I'm a smart kid with a good imagination, but I just need to DO something with it.

Listen, I'm not proud of myself for lying, but trust me, I'm not the ONLY one in this family who bends the truth.

I've heard grown-ups lie ten times a week, but if you ask me I'll bet it's even MORE than that.

The first time I remember Mom telling me a lie was when I was about three years old and she had me try broccoli.

And Mom doesn't seem to have any problem lying to MANNY, either.

Last December, when Mom put the gingerbread house out on the kitchen table, she told Manny not to touch it until Christmas or it would turn into a million spiders, which is kind of a crazy thing to tell a little kid. But it backfired when Manny fumigated the gingerbread house with a can of bug spray.

Dad's a pretty honest guy in general, but even HE fibs when it's convenient for him.

Dad used to HATE it when the ice cream truck came through our neighborhood, because me and Rodrick would always start begging him for money as soon as we heard the music.

So Dad told us the ice cream truck only plays music when they're OUT of ice cream.

I actually think lying might be inherited, because GRANDPA does it, too. But he should've gotten his stories straight with Dad, because Grandpa used to say the ice cream truck driver was a clown who spanked children he caught roaming around outside.

I'm kind of embarrassed to say that when Grandpa first told me that, I actually BELIEVED him.

So I felt like it was my responsibility to get the word out to OTHER kids in the neighborhood.

I've learned not to trust the grown-ups in our family, but nobody's done more to mess with my head than RODRICK.

The first lie I can remember him telling me was that if your belly button got untied, your BUTT would fall off.

I made sure my preschool classmates knew about that, which caused a big stir at school.

Right around this same time Rodrick told me that the outer ring of the toilet seat was only used by girls, and that guys are supposed to lift the seat no matter WHAT.

I believed him, and if I hadn't accidentally left the door unlocked one night, I might've gone on using the toilet the wrong way for the rest of my life.

Sometimes Rodrick told me things that got me in BIG trouble. When I was in second grade he said that if a person wears camouflage, they're actually INVISIBLE to everyone else.

That one got me banned from the town pool for the rest of the summer.

A lot of Rodrick's lies ended up costing me MONEY, too. One year Rodrick told me that if I dug a hole and put all my birthday money in it, a tree would grow and I could get cash from it whenever I WANTED.

That seemed like a pretty sweet deal to ME.

124

So I did what he said, and I even watered it twice a day. But when I told Mom my Money Tree wasn't growing, she got a shovel and dug up the hole, which was EMPTY.

I'm glad Mom stepped in when she did, because in another day or two all of my birthday money would've been spent on bubble gum and comic books.

Sometimes Rodrick just took my money outright.

Once, when I lost one of my baby teeth, I put it under my pillow for the tooth fairy. But when I went to see if she left me fifty cents, I found a note that I'm pretty sure Rodrick wrote himself.

SORRY I'M LIGHT ON CASH TONIGHT. I WILL HOOK YOU UP NEXT TIME.

—T.F.

Rodrick told me the tooth fairy was only ONE of the fairies that comes in the middle of the night and gives money. He said there was an arm fairy and a leg fairy and a bunch of other ones, too.

Rodrick said that when you get older your child arms and legs fall off, and when they do, you put them under your pillow and get money.

126

He said after THAT, your adult limbs start growing in, but sometimes a kid's arms or legs get loose and the adult ones come in early.

I was TERRIFIED that was gonna happen to ME, so I checked every night to make sure my arms and legs were on tight.

Rodrick was always coming up with ways to scare me. Back when our basement wasn't finished, there were open gaps under the stair treads.

Rodrick said if I went up the stairs too slow, a monster would grab my ankle. From then on, I started taking the stairs two at a time.

After I got good at THAT, I tried taking the stairs THREE at a time. But I guess that was a little too ambitious.

Eventually we finished the basement and the gaps were covered up with wood. But GRAMMA'S basement is still unfinished, and before I go down there I usually make sure everything's all clear first.

Another thing Rodrick said to scare me was that if I burped indoors, the ghost of George Washington would haunt me. I have no idea how he came up with THAT one, but it still makes me think twice before opening a can of soda.

Sometimes Rodrick would tell me
something that actually COULD be true,
and that's when things got confusing.

He told me once that if a person sleeps with
their mouth open they'll eat an average of
five spiders a night, which is kind of
believable if you think about it.

Another time Rodrick told me that it's
dangerous to wake someone up when
they're sleepwalking. I thought there could
be a chance he was actually telling the truth,
because I'm pretty sure I heard that one
somewhere else.

130

But then a few nights later I caught Rodrick eating an ice cream sandwich that was supposed to be MINE and I realized it was just another one of his dirty tricks.

I've been lied to so much over the years, it could take me the rest of my life to figure out what's true and what's not.

In the meantime, I'm not taking any chances.

<u>Thursday</u>

Mom's only been going to school for a few days now, but she's acting like a COMPLETELY different person. When she gets home at night, she's always in a good mood. She doesn't even get mad if I haven't finished my chores.

Mom says she's happy because she's being challenged at school, and the rest of us should try learning new things, too.

But I have a theory when it comes to this sort of thing. I figure your brain only has so much space in it, and by the time you're eight or nine years old, it's all filled up.

So if you want to learn something new after THAT, you have to make room by getting rid of something OLD.

I figure that's why school gets harder the further you go. Every time new information comes in, your brain automatically clears out something ELSE to make space.

To prove my point, ever since I learned about photosynthesis in Science, I haven't been able to remember how to do long division.

Question 1: What is 367 divided by 12? Remember to show your work!

NO CLUE.

I just wish you could CHOOSE what your brain gets rid of. I've completely forgotten the cheat codes for Twisted Wizard, but I still have a really clear memory of the time I scared Dad when he came out of the shower.

And believe me, I'd pay good money to wipe THAT image from my memory bank.

Mom says me and Rodrick need to start thinking about what we want to do when we grow up and start planning for the future NOW. She says when you're a kid you should do as many things as you can to find out what you like so that later you'll know what to focus on.

I already KNOW what I want to do for my career. I'm planning on being a video game tester when I grow up. The way I see it, I've been training for that job ever since I was old enough to hold a controller in my hands.

But whenever I tell Mom my plan, she doesn't seem excited about it.

Mom says I should set my sights HIGHER and become an engineer or a doctor or something like that. She says if I just play video games all day and don't take school seriously, I'm gonna end up being a garbage collector.

First of all, the only doctor I know is our pediatrician, Dr. Higgins, and I can't see myself spending the rest of my life suctioning mucus out of little kids' noses.

And second, being a garbage collector seems like a pretty sweet deal to ME. The guys who collect our trash get to be outside every day and crank their music up really loud. So if the video game tester thing doesn't work out for me, garbage collector seems like a good fallback plan.

When I was little, Mom always told me I could be anything I wanted when I grew up.

I didn't find out until later on that she was just talking about JOBS. I thought I could literally be ANYTHING.

Mom's always saying we have a lot of brains in our family, and that one of my great-great-great aunts helped invent a cure for a disease way back when.

But trust me, we've got a lot of real DUMMIES in our family, too. Just last week my uncle Gary cut down a big branch that was overhanging his driveway, and he ended up breaking his collarbone.

With people like Uncle Gary in my gene pool, it's a miracle I can even tie my own shoes. But Mom's always saying I can do great things if I put my mind to it.

Albert Sandy says human beings only use 80% of our brains, and if we can tap into the OTHER 20%, we can do amazing things.

If I'm the one who figures out how to tap into that extra 20%, though, I'm keeping that knowledge to myself. Because if you have all these people going around using their brains at full capacity, it's gonna be totally bananas.

<u>Wednesday</u>

Mom's been trying to get Rodrick excited about college, and said it's time for him to get serious about looking into schools.

But Rodrick's still convinced his band is gonna make it big and that college is just a waste of time for a guy like him. I think Mom's starting to get a little worried, because now she's making Rodrick research colleges for a half hour a day instead of doing chores.

Rodrick wrote to a handful of schools to ask for their brochures, and Mom got all excited when they came in the mail. But most of the colleges were for DOGS, which either Rodrick didn't notice or he thinks those might be the only schools he has a chance of getting into.

140

Since Mom can't get Rodrick interested in college, she's turned her attention to ME. On Monday, Mom took me to her school so I could see what the campus was like, and I have to admit it was actually kind of cool.

Mom said that in college you can study anything you WANT, and all you need to succeed is a "curious mind." She told me that, while she went to her class, I should explore the campus so I could get a sense of what it's like for students.

I walked around for a while, but I felt like I didn't belong there.

Eventually I went to the library and just waited for Mom to be finished with her class.

I started doing my homework, but I could tell that all the college kids were wondering what some middle schooler was doing in their library.

That's when I remembered hearing about
a girl my age who's so smart, she's already
in medical school studying to be a doctor.
I figured if I made myself look really smart,
I'd look like I BELONGED there.

So I grabbed a stack of thick books about
psychology off the nearest shelf and
pretended I was really into them.

A few minutes later, a girl pulled up a chair
and started talking to me.

The girl said I looked smart and she wanted to know if I'd be willing to tutor her for her Psychology test she had later in the week.

Now, I don't know the first thing about psychology, but I realized an opportunity like THIS only comes up once in a lifetime. I told her I was kind of busy at the moment, but I'd be willing to tutor her the NEXT day.

When Mom came back from class, I used her library card to check out every book on psychology I could find. And that night I studied like I've never studied before.

When the next day rolled around, I was READY. I asked Mom if she'd take me back to her college, and she seemed thrilled.

144

I spent two hours helping that girl prepare for her test, and by the time we were done, I knew she'd get a good grade. But then this big guy came by who was apparently her BOYFRIEND. And believe me, if I'd known there was a boyfriend involved I wouldn't have killed myself learning a bunch of useless information.

If this is the kind of thing I can expect in college, I'm gonna have to PASS. And by the way, I was right about what happens when you learn new stuff. I had a test on world capitals today, and I couldn't remember a single one.

Monday

All anyone at school can talk about these days is Mariana Mendoza's Halloween party, which is this coming Friday. But it's a little annoying for me, because I won't be getting an invitation.

Mariana's parties are kind of legendary because her parents don't care WHAT goes on, as long as it stays in the basement.

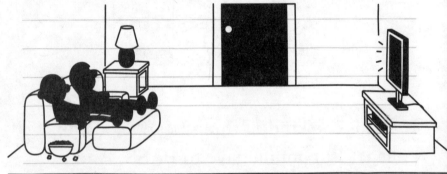

Last year's party got TOTALLY out of control. It started OFF in the basement, but so many people showed up that it spilled out into the yard, and the cops came to shut it down. And that's a pretty big deal for a middle school party.

This year, Mariana's parents said she has to keep it SMALL, so she's only inviting people who are in the school band with her. That's bad news for kids like me who were hoping to get invited this time around.

Rowley's gonna get invited, though, because he's in the band. But believe me, if he goes to a party like THAT, he's gonna be in over his head.

I was thinking about this at school today
when I had a genius idea. If I join the
BAND, I can get invited to Mariana's
party.

Tonight, when I told Mom and Dad I
wanted to join the band, Mom was all for it.
She was really excited I wanted to challenge
myself and try something new. But Dad
wasn't crazy about the idea.

Dad said instruments are EXPENSIVE,
and he doesn't think I'll stick with it. But
Mom said Rodrick stuck with the DRUMS,
which I don't think really helped my case.

That's when Dad brought up the PIANO.

Two years ago, Mom saw me fooling around with one of those little electronic keyboards at the mall the week before Christmas. I liked it because it had all these buttons that made different sound effects.

I think Mom got a little overly excited that I was showing interest in a musical instrument, because on Christmas Eve a truck rolled up to deliver a full-size piano.

Judging by Dad's reaction, I don't think
Mom checked with him before buying it.

At first I was excited about the piano, but
when I realized it didn't make laser sounds
and stuff like that, I lost interest real quick.

But Mom wasn't gonna let me give up so
fast. She hired a lady named Mrs. French
to come to the house and give me private
lessons twice a week.

Mrs. French knew her stuff when it came to the piano, but I was a TERRIBLE student.

The first problem was Mrs. French's teaching style. She'd sit right behind me on the bench and put her fingers on top of MY fingers. That approach might work for SOME of Mrs. French's students, but it definitely didn't work for ME.

Then there was the music itself. If I was gonna play the piano, I wanted to learn cool songs like the ones you hear on the radio. But Mrs. French said I had to start with the BASICS, and she gave me a "Beginner's Songbook" that looked like it was older than Mrs. French.

All the songs in that thing were really corny, and it was hard for me to get into them.

C-D-E with Bee

C D E!   Sing with me!

Sing with bee!   Sing with glee!

I felt pretty bad, because Mrs. French gave me homework every time she visited, but I NEVER practiced in between lessons. So every time she came we'd have to start over with the "C-D-E" song, which must've driven her nuts.

Eventually Mrs. French gave up trying to teach me anything, and she'd just read gossip magazines while I did my own thing.

It went on like that for a month or two, but eventually Mom discovered what was happening and that was the end of my private lessons.

Now the piano is just a giant piece of furniture taking up space in the living room. I think Mom and Dad are still paying that thing off, so I can kind of understand why Dad's not eager for me to try a NEW instrument.

Luckily, Mom had my back. She said maybe the piano wasn't the right FIT for me, and that sometimes the instrument needs to find the PERSON. She finally convinced him when she said that kids who play musical instruments do better at math and go on to get better jobs.

A half hour later we were at the music store
downtown picking out an instrument.

My number one requirement for an
instrument is that it makes me look COOL.
I saw a guy at Mom's college strumming a
guitar outside the library, and he
DEFINITELY had the right idea.

Unfortunately, the guitar isn't one of the instruments in our middle school band. So I had to pick something else.

I had my eye on the saxophone at first, because with that one it's hard NOT to look cool. I learned THAT from Declan Vaughn, who practices his during recess.

But there are WAY too many buttons on that thing, and I knew I'd never get the hang of it.

Mom suggested I take a look at the French horn, which SHE used to play as a kid. The French horn looked cool enough and only had three buttons, so I figured I could probably handle it.

The shopkeeper pulled the French horn down off the hook and handed it to me. But when Dad saw the price tag, he put the brakes on the whole thing.

Dad said we should RENT instead of buy, because that would be a whole lot cheaper. But all the rental instruments were USED.

The kid who played the French horn in the school band last year was Joshua Ballard, and there was a chance the rental belonged to HIM.

Mom and Dad got into an argument in front of everyone, and it was kind of embarrassing. Dad said we were spending too much money on something I'd quit in two weeks, and Mom said he needed to show more FAITH in me.

Eventually, Dad caved in. But before he swiped his credit card, he made me promise I'd practice every night.

This thing better be as easy as it looks. Because it feels like a lot of trouble to go through just to get invited to a Halloween party.

Tuesday
When I was picking an instrument, I should've put more thought into it. I was mostly thinking about IMAGE, but there are OTHER considerations, too.

It was a pain in the neck bringing my French horn to school today, because the CASE weighs almost as much as the instrument. But when I saw what Grayden Bundy had to deal with, I felt OK about my choice.

Everybody says Annabelle Grier is one of the smartest girls in our grade, and it's easy to see why. She plays the piccolo, so she's not wasting any energy lugging a heavy instrument around.

But George Deveney might be even smarter than HER. He plays the kettledrums, and those are too big to take home every night, so they stay in the band room full-time.

Something I never really noticed before is that most of the kids in the band actually kind of LOOK like their instruments. I don't know if people do that on purpose or if it's just a coincidence.

The great thing about the band is that there are no tryouts or anything. Basically, if you buy an instrument and show up, you're in.

But I wasn't thinking it all the way through when I picked my instrument. The French horn is in the brass section, and almost everyone in the brass section is a GUY.

The woodwind section is the complete opposite. It's all GIRLS except for a handful of guys, including Rowley. I really wish he'd given me a heads-up about it, because that information would've been nice to know.

Maybe Rowley didn't tell me on PURPOSE so I wouldn't give him any competition.

I noticed he sits right next to Mariana Mendoza, and believe me, that's no accident.

When class started, Mrs. Graziano told us to start warming up. That's when I remembered that my least favorite sound in the world is kids practicing their instruments.

But Mrs. Graziano didn't seem to mind. She's retiring this year, so I think she's already checked out.

I sat next to the only other kid who plays the French horn, Evan Pittman, who looked like he knew what he was doing. With the way he moved his fingers around, it seemed a lot more complicated than I was expecting. But I figured I might as well give it a shot.

I filled my cheeks with air just like Evan did, and I blew into the mouthpiece as hard as I could. But the air didn't come out where I expected.

As soon as it happened, everyone in the band just FROZE. Jake McGough started trying to sniff out who did it, because he's got a weird talent for that sort of thing.

But if there's one thing you should know about me, it's that I have NEVER taken blame for a fart. I'd even throw my own mother under the bus, and trust me, I have.

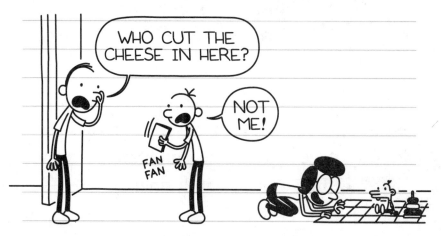

The kids in the band were starting to look my way. I was really sweating it, because if I was gonna get invited to Mariana Mendoza's Halloween party, my reputation couldn't take a hit like this.

Jake McGough was getting closer and closer, and I knew I was only seconds away from getting identified.

So I did what I HAD to do, and pinned it on Grayden Bundy.

I didn't feel TOO bad, because Grayden has a reputation for letting it rip in class. So the way I see it, this was punishment for all the times he got away with one.

<u>Thursday</u>

I wish I could go back in time and pick a new instrument, because this French horn is no joke.

The guy at the music store never mentioned that it's a LEFT-handed instrument, and I'm a RIGHTY.

I thought it would be easy with the whole three-button thing, but my left hand isn't strong enough to work it. Plus, the mouthpiece is TINY, and I can't get any air through it. So far I haven't been able to squeeze out ANYTHING that sounds like a musical note.

Unfortunately, that doesn't help me with DAD. He wants to hear me practicing each night, like I promised him.

Luckily, I found some video clips of a high school girl practicing HER French horn. So those videos are doing the trick, at least for now.

This whole musical instrument thing might be a big waste of time, anyway. Mariana didn't invite the entire band to her party tomorrow night, just the WOODWIND section.

That means if you play a brass instrument like me, you're out of luck. But then I realized I've got an IN. Rowley's part of the woodwind section, and if HE'S going, then I can just tag along.

I can't just show up with him, though, or I could get turned away at the door.

So I figured out a way to make sure that doesn't happen. I realized that if I make myself part of Rowley's COSTUME, then wherever he goes, I go, too. That's how I came up with the idea of us going as a two-headed monster.

On the walk home from school, I told Rowley all about my plan.

But Rowley said he wanted to go to the party as a "nice witch," and his mom was already working on his costume.

See, this is EXACTLY why Rowley needs me to go with him.

I told Rowley if he went to a party like this dressed up as a witch, he'd never live it down at school. I think that made him kind of nervous, so he said he changed his mind and wanted to do the two-headed-monster thing I had come up with.

So tonight we got to work making the costume out of some sheets I found in the linen closet. When Mom got home from school, I realized I should've asked permission before cutting them up. But she was really happy me and Rowley were MAKING something instead of playing video games like we usually do.

I told her we were making a two-headed-monster costume, and she thought that was a GREAT idea for trick-or-treating.

168

I told Mom the costume was actually for Mariana Mendoza's Halloween party, and as soon as I said it, I wished I could take it back. Like I said before, last year's party was a total blowout, and EVERYONE in our town heard about it.

But Mom was actually good with the idea. She said a party was a chance for us to "branch out" and grow our "friend circle." She said she'd even be happy to give us a RIDE.

I'm just relieved she didn't suggest adding another head to the costume, because believe me, that's EXACTLY the kind of thing she would think of.

SHUDDER

Halloween

It took a long time to get to Mariana's house tonight because the street was full of little kids trick-or-treating.

I was kind of GLAD we were a little late, because if we showed up right on time, we'd look like we were too eager. When we finally got to Mariana's, I told Mom thanks for the ride and not to come back for us until the party ended at 11:00.

But Mom turned off the ignition, got out of the minivan, and pulled some bags from the back.

When I asked her what she was doing, she said she was coming in to introduce herself to Mr. and Mrs. Mendoza.

I BEGGED Mom not to, but when she decides to do something, there's really no stopping her.

She rang the doorbell, but nobody answered. We could hear loud music coming from the basement, so Mom opened the door and we all stepped inside.

Mr. and Mrs. Mendoza were on the couch watching a horror movie, and they didn't seem too interested in getting up and chatting with Mom.

Mom asked if she could go downstairs and check out the party, and they seemed totally fine with it.

Now I was REALLY nervous. Mom opened the door to the basement and headed on down, and all me and Rowley could really do was follow. There were a lot of kids there already, and they looked like they were having a blast.

But when everyone saw Mom, they stopped what they were doing.

Mom pulled a bunch of homemade Halloween games out of her bag, and I got a sick feeling in my stomach. I should've known what Mom was up to when I saw her reading the October edition of "Family Frolic" magazine last night.

When Mom pulled out her party games, I figured everyone would just ignore her and go back to having fun. But then something CRAZY happened.

A bunch of the girls started HELPING Mom set up her stuff.

From that point on Mom was running the show. She invited everyone at the party to play these corny Halloween games. I thought I might actually die of embarrassment, but everybody got into it and seemed to be having a great time.

BONK

I think the person who was having the MOST fun was Rowley. His favorite game was the one where you eat a doughnut on a string, and he set the record with five in thirty seconds.

Once I realized everyone was having a good time, I relaxed a little. I even played a few games MYSELF. Me and Rowley took first prize in Pin the Boo on the Ghost, and I gotta admit we made a pretty good team.

In fact, we won a LOT of Mom's games. The only one we stunk at was the Mini Pumpkin Toss, but I guess you can't be good at EVERYTHING.

After the games were over, somebody turned the music louder, and the party cranked up a notch. It was a little hard to pull out my best moves while I was attached to Rowley, but I still had some pretty good stuff.

I gotta say, it was AWESOME. The only kids
who WEREN'T having fun were the handful
of guys who were there. But I wasn't gonna
let a few sour grapes spoil my good time.

Right when the party was about to hit the
next level, Rowley told me he needed to
use the bathroom. But when we made the
costume we didn't PLAN for that sort of
thing.

There wasn't a zipper or anything like that,
so the only way to get out of the costume
was to cut it off. Neither one of us was
wearing pants underneath, so THAT
wasn't happening.

I was pretty annoyed, because earlier in the evening I had TOLD Rowley to slow down on the fruit punch, and of course he hadn't listened.

I decided he was just gonna have to wait until we got home to deal with it. So I tried to go back to having fun, but Rowley made it kind of impossible for me to enjoy myself.

I think Mom figured out what was going on from the look on Rowley's face, and she said it was time for us to "wrap things up" and head home.

Now I was REALLY mad. The party was in full swing and we had to leave because Rowley needed a potty break.

But Mom said it's better to leave a party when it's going strong than when it's fizzling out. She said it makes you look COOL, because everybody will think you have better things to do.

I don't know what's better than hanging out with Mariana Mendoza, but Mom was practically pushing me up the stairs.

When we drove away, I was pretty miserable. But Mom was as happy as I've ever seen her.

Thursday

All this week, Mariana and her friends have been saying how great the party was and how much fun my mom was. I don't know how to feel about that, exactly, but I guess I'll take it as a compliment.

I've kind of lost interest in being in the band, though, and it's not JUST because the party's in the rearview mirror. Once we got back to school on Monday, the guys in the woodwind section started giving me a hard time.

And it's not just the BIG guys, either. Even Jake McGough's gotten in on the act.

When I told Mom and Dad I was thinking of quitting the band, Dad said that wasn't an option. He said my instrument cost a lot of money, and that I had to honor my "commitment."

He said I can't just quit something because it's HARD, and if there's anything he's gonna teach me, it's PERSEVERANCE.

I could tell Dad wasn't gonna let it go, so I promised him I'd keep trying. He seemed pretty happy with that, and I thought I was off the hook.

Then he told me he's gonna come to the Fall Concert to cheer me on. I told Dad the concert is during the school day, so he won't be ABLE to come. But Dad said it's important to him, so he's gonna take off work.

Now the pressure's REALLY on. I've been trying to learn to play this thing ever since, but trust me, it's not easy.

I asked Rowley to come over and help me tonight, because I figured he's been in the band for a while and knows a thing or two about instruments. But every time the two of us are in a room together, we end up getting distracted.

Dad was pretty mad, because he said all me and Rowley do when we're together is screw around. So he sent Rowley home and told me to get back to work. But even that girl in the videos gave up trying to learn the French horn, so I guess I'm REALLY on my own.

Wednesday
Today was the day of the big Fall Concert. I never technically learned how to play my instrument, but I did figure out how to get BY.

I sit right next to Evan Pittman in band practice, and he can play his French horn just fine. I realized if I just piggybacked on him and PRETENDED I was playing, he could do the work for BOTH of us.

So that's what I've been doing for the past two weeks. And if Mrs. Graziano didn't notice from ten feet away, I knew DAD wouldn't notice from across the room.

But ten minutes before showtime, Evan was nowhere to be found. I asked his best friend, Marcus Perez, where Evan was, and Marcus said Evan was getting his braces off today and was going to miss the concert.

I couldn't BELIEVE Evan would hang me out to dry like that. I thought the brass section is supposed to have each other's BACKS.

When it came time for the band to do warm-ups, I started to SWEAT.

I was praying Dad forgot about the Fall Concert, but then there he was at the stage door.

After the audience took their seats, it was time to go on stage. Mrs. Graziano led us out in single file, with the brass section going next to last.

But the woodwinds were right behind us, and that idiot Jake McGough stepped on the back of my shoe and gave me a flat tire.

I had to put my horn down to fix my
shoe, and when I did, the last kid in the
woodwind section went through the stage
door and let it shut behind him.

I tried to open the door, but it was
LOCKED, so I pounded on the window.
But everyone was tuning their instruments
and couldn't hear me.

The concert was about to start, and all I could think about was Dad looking at my empty chair. So I knocked HARDER.

Luckily, Rowley saw me at the window, got up from his chair, and opened the door. But then he stepped INSIDE the room and let the door shut BEHIND him.

Now we were BOTH stuck. I knocked on the window again, but right at that moment Mrs. Graziano struck up the band and everyone started playing. Now it was HOPELESS, because there was no way anyone was gonna hear me with George Deveney pounding away on his kettledrums.

When the clarinet section piped in, Rowley
went into a PANIC. He started playing
along with the rest of the band, which was
DEFINITELY not helping matters.

It was pretty clear it was gonna be up to me
to get us out of there. I tried to pry the door
open by putting my foot on the wall and
pulling on the handle with all my strength.
But I guess my pants couldn't take the stress.

I looked in the mirror on the back wall to check the damage, and there was a five-inch tear down the middle of my pants. That was really bad news, because you could see my underwear.

I realized that even if we managed to get the door back open, I couldn't go out there with this giant HOLE in my pants. So I looked around the room to see if there was anything I could use to cover up. I found a black binder on Mrs. Graziano's desk, and I slipped it down the back of my pants.

The binder covered up the hole pretty well, and from a distance no one would be able to notice. But it was so STIFF, I couldn't actually sit DOWN. So I had to take it out and come up with a different idea.

Then I thought of a solution. I grabbed a black marker off Mrs. Graziano's desk and told Rowley to color in the part of my underwear that was showing. That way, no one would even know my pants ripped.

Unfortunately, that's right when DAD came through the door. I don't know what it looked like to HIM, but I have a feeling it didn't look GOOD.

<u>Thursday</u>

No matter how many times I explained to Dad what had happened at the Fall Concert, he didn't want to hear it. He said me and Rowley were goofing off when we should've been performing with the band, and that's all he needed to know.

My punishment is two weeks with no television or video games, and I'm not allowed to have friends over after school. The only thing I really CAN do is practice my French horn, which I guess is the point.

But practicing that thing stresses me out, and stress makes me HUNGRY. I usually have a whole pillowcase full of candy at this time of year, but since I skipped trick-or-treating to go to that party, I missed out on the best part of Halloween.

I knew there had to be leftover candy somewhere in the house, because on Halloween night, Dad told Mom the geese chased all the trick-or-treaters away.

So after school today I looked in all the places I thought Mom might've stashed the candy, but I came up empty. Now I was REALLY craving something sweet, but the only thing in the pantry was a bag of chocolate chips Mom told us were off-limits.

I think she's planning on making chocolate-chip cookies for the church Bake Fair. But I figured she'd never notice if just ONE chip went missing.

So I got some scissors and cut a tiny chocolate-chip-size hole in the bottom of the bag. Well, one chocolate chip turned into two, and two turned into FOUR. Then I kind of just lost my mind.

When I was done, I must've eaten at least a quarter of the bag. I thought there was still a chance Mom wouldn't notice, but the hole in the bag had gotten a lot BIGGER, and I needed to do something about that.

So I went through the junk drawer to look for a stapler.

But before I could USE it, the bottom of the bag totally gave out.

I stapled the bag shut and recovered as many chips as I could off the floor. But I kind of couldn't help myself, and a lot of them never made it back into the bag.

Now there was no WAY Mom wasn't gonna notice. I was already in enough trouble, and I really didn't need to add to my problems. So I called Rowley for help.

194

I told him my situation, and how I needed him to bring me as many chocolate chips as he could.

Rowley showed up at my front door five minutes later, and he was all out of breath. He said he would've gotten to my house SOONER, but the geese were out on our street and he had to cut through my neighbor's backyard to steer clear of them.

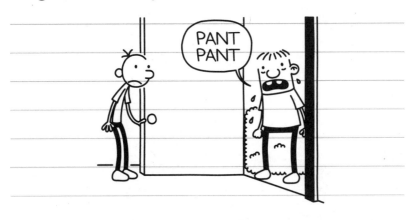

I asked Rowley for the chocolate chips, and he opened his hands. But they were useless because they were completely MELTED.

I told Rowley he was gonna have to go back and get MORE, but he said that was all they had. He said maybe he could call up Scotty Douglas down the street to see if HE had any chocolate chips, and that sounded like a pretty good plan to me.

But when Rowley picked up the phone, I noticed he was leaving chocolaty fingerprints EVERYWHERE.

I knew if Dad found ONE of Rowley's fingerprints in the kitchen, I was dead. So we got some paper towels and started wiping down the whole kitchen.

When we ran out of paper towels, I went
into the laundry room to get some more.
But when I did, I made a HUGE discovery.

I found Mom's entire stash of leftover
Halloween candy tucked behind the rolls of
paper towels.

There were five unopened bags in there,
and it was ALL stuff I like.

I figured I'd give Rowley a few packets of gummy worms for helping me out with the cleanup. But I couldn't resist taking the opportunity to play a little prank on him first.

I thought Rowley would laugh, but he was TERRIFIED. Even AFTER I showed him the worm was just a piece of candy, he still couldn't get over it.

That's when a lightbulb went on over my head. People LOVE to be scared, and if you're good at it, you can make a FORTUNE. It can't be that hard, either. I.M. Spooky is filthy rich, and that guy doesn't even EXIST.

I heard about these college kids who made a horror movie, and they only spent a couple hundred bucks filming it. Then they sold the movie to a big studio, and now those guys are MILLIONAIRES.

If those guys could do it, so could I. And I didn't need hundreds of dollars, either. All I needed was a couple of bags of gummy worms and Mom and Dad's old camcorder.

I could already see the movie poster in my mind.

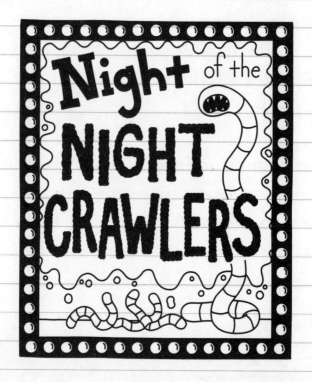

And when my movie wins Best Picture, I'll be sure to thank all the little people who helped me along the way.

The person who'll deserve the BIGGEST thanks is MOM. She's the one who's always saying I should use my imagination and do something creative, so when I'm a famous director I'll bet she'll be proud.

Before all THAT could happen, though, we needed to get started making this movie. I told Rowley my idea to make a film where man-eating worms terrorize a town, but that seemed to make him nervous. He said maybe we could switch out the worms for something less SCARY, like butterflies.

THAT TICKLES!

But I told him nobody was gonna pay good money to see a movie like THAT. I said we could have some funny parts so it wasn't JUST scary, and he seemed to warm up to the idea.

Rowley wanted to get started filming right then and there, but I told him we weren't doing anything without a SCRIPT. So we went upstairs, turned on my computer, and got to work.

NIGHT OF THE
NIGHT CRAWLERS

Written by
Greg Heffley

Based on a concept by
Greg Heffley

Rowley said HE wanted to write, too, but I really didn't want to share credit on this thing since it was MY idea. So I told him he could do the storyboards, which are little drawings that show how each camera shot is supposed to look.

I figured a good way to start the movie would be to show a married couple having an ordinary day BEFORE the worms started attacking.

EVENING. A man comes home from work in a good mood, whistling a cheery tune. He opens the side door and steps inside the kitchen.

But I ran into a problem right away. I was planning on directing, and Rowley was our only actor. That meant we couldn't really show two characters on the screen at the same time.

The other problem was that I didn't want it to be too obvious that Rowley was playing all the parts, or people might think our film was low-budget. So I had to get a little creative.

HUSBAND
Hi, dear. I am home
from work.

WIFE
Hello, honey. I hope you don't
mind if I don't turn around but
I am really concentrating on
doing these dishes.

HUSBAND
That's OK. I am gonna
go upstairs and take
a shower.

WIFE
Good, I can smell
you from here! (laughs)

I felt like there was already a little too much talking, so it was time to get to the action.

UPSTAIRS BATHROOM. The man steps inside the shower and turns the water on.
                    HUSBAND
         Oh, man! This shower
       is gonna feel GREAT! And
        my wife is right about
             me stinking.

But then WORMS shoot out of the showerhead!

HUSBAND

What the heck? This isn't
water! It's WORMS!

But these are no ordinary worms.
They are man-eating NIGHT
CRAWLERS!

HUSBAND

Oh, great! These things
are actually EATING me!

Worms come out of the man's eyes
and nose.

When Rowley finished that last drawing, he was white as a ghost. But I reminded him the worms were just candy, and that calmed him down.

BACK TO THE KITCHEN. The man runs into the room with a towel around his waist.

                HUSBAND
        Honey! Don't use the
             water! It's --

But it's TOO LATE. The woman is a skeleton.

Now I REALLY started to lose Rowley. I had to remind him this was all make-believe, and we had a plastic skeleton that we were gonna use for this scene. But he was practically hyperventilating.

I realized maybe this was a good place to add some comedy, so I put in a line of dialogue, and that brought Rowley right back.

HUSBAND
Well, I guess this
means I'm single! (winks)

After that was taken care of, it was back to the action. And the next scene was a BIG one.

The man looks outside. The house is totally surrounded by night crawlers.

HUSBAND
Oh no! I'm surrounded!
I'd better call the COPS!

The man puts the phone to his ear and dials 911.

                    HUSBAND
        Hello, is this the police?
        I am calling to report...
            Wait, WHAT THE -- ?

A worm crawls from the phone
into the man's ear and out the
other one.

                    HUSBAND
        AIIEEEEEEE!(dies)

After I finished writing that scene, I realized
this was taking too much time. Plus, there
were some scenes I hadn't figured out
how to shoot yet, like the battle between
the mayor and the 500-foot King Night
Crawler at the end of the movie.

Since we weren't gonna get this whole thing done in one day, I decided we might as well get started and shoot the scenes we just wrote.

I found my parents' camcorder in Mom's closet, and luckily there was a film cartridge in the camera bag. We also borrowed some clothes from Dad's closet for Rowley's first costume, and even though the pants were a little long, they more or less fit.

We shot the opening scene, which took about three times longer than it should've because Rowley had trouble remembering his lines.

After that, it was time to film Rowley as the guy's wife.

Rowley wasn't comfortable wearing one of Mom's dresses, so we settled on some yoga pants. We didn't have a wig, so Rowley wore a hoodie to cover his head.

It wasn't exactly like I had imagined it, but sometimes you have to just keep things moving.

After we wrapped things up in the kitchen, we went upstairs to film the bathroom scenes. Rowley didn't want to get his hair wet, so he wore a shower cap we found underneath Mom's sink. I found Dad's bathing suit in one of his dresser drawers, and Rowley put that on and got in the shower.

It turns out the shower scene was A LOT harder to film than I expected. I had to shoot Rowley from the waist up so you couldn't see that he was wearing a bathing suit. Plus, I hadn't really thought through how to make it look like worms were coming out of the shower head, and nothing I did looked right.

Eventually I settled on just throwing worms at Rowley's face. Hopefully it'll look realistic when it's all edited together.

I couldn't find where Mom kept her food coloring, so we had to settle for some ketchup for the blood. It was a little too thick, but it wasn't the worst thing in the world, either.

After we wrapped things up in the bathroom, it was time to go back down to the kitchen. We shot the skeleton scene pretty quickly, and the hoodie added something extra to it.

At this point it was getting a little late, and
I was worried we weren't gonna finish
shooting our scenes before my parents got
home. So we hurried outside and got to
work spreading the gummy worms around
the yard.

But I wasn't satisfied with how this scene
was coming out. There just weren't enough
worms to make it look scary.

I decided we were gonna have to dip into the other bag of gummy worms to make the scene work. But when I opened the door to the laundry room, I got a nasty surprise.

I was trying to figure out what to do with the pig when I heard Rowley screaming in the kitchen. So I ran out to see what was wrong.

A bunch of geese were going to TOWN on our gummy worms, so I opened the door to try to scare them off. But they wouldn't budge.

Once the geese finished off the gummy worms, they wanted MORE. I closed the door, and me and Rowley hid under the kitchen table to try to figure out our next move.

I told Rowley the only thing geese are scared of are other ANIMALS. But before I could say another word, Rowley was at the window with Manny's See-and-Talk.

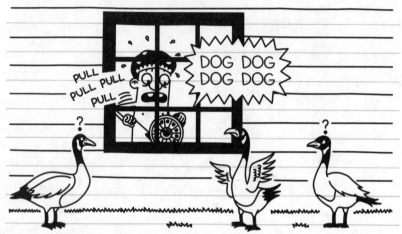

Now the geese were pecking at the windows, and I was scared that if we didn't do something, they might actually break IN. That's when I remembered that the last time Rodrick went trick-or-treating, he wore this awful wolf mask, which was still down in the basement.

I figured if ANYTHING was gonna scare these geese off, it was THAT.

Me and Rowley ran down to the furnace room to find the mask. The old Halloween costumes were in a box on the fourth shelf, so it was a two-man job to get it down.

I got up on Rowley's shoulders and reached for the box, but when I DID I knocked a snow globe off the shelf. And when THAT happened, the WITCH went off.

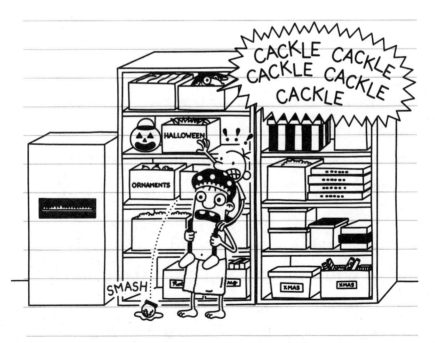

I grabbed on to the shelf, and the whole storage unit came crashing down.

When the dust settled, we were both lucky to be ALIVE. Once Rowley got free, he shot out of the basement so fast, I think he might've actually taken the stairs FOUR at a time.

And once he got out of the house, Rowley didn't STOP. He climbed halfway up the big tree on the side of the house, and that's where I found him, babbling nonsense.

I tried to talk him into coming down, but he wouldn't budge. So I got a tennis racket and some balls and tried to KNOCK him down, but that only made him climb HIGHER.

220

Unfortunately for me, that's the moment
Dad came home.

Wednesday

It's been a pretty crazy couple of weeks
since me and Rowley made our movie. I've
been too busy to keep up with my journal,
because Dad has had me working in the
furnace room every night sorting through
all the stuff that fell off the shelves.

I tried explaining to Dad that we were just making a movie and things got out of hand, but it was like talking to a wall. I thought Mom would be a little more understanding, but it turns out the tape in the camcorder was of Manny taking his first steps, and we recorded right over it.

So I'm stuck cleaning up this mess in the furnace room, and meanwhile, Rowley is drinking in his newfound fame. A news crew came out and recorded the moment when the fire department got him down out of the tree, and the footage of the "dramatic rescue" spread like crazy.

Rowley hasn't even been back to school, because every morning talk show wants a piece of him.

What's really annoying is that in all these
interviews, Rowley hasn't mentioned my
name ONCE, even though I'm the one
who MADE him famous. But these days
he pretty much acts like the world revolves
around him.

I guess that's what fame does to a person.
All I can say is, you'd never see ME making
a fool out of myself just to get a cheap laugh
from the people watching at home.

ACKNOWLEDGMENTS

Thanks to all the Wimpy Kid fans for encouraging me to write about Greg Heffley and his crazy family. Thanks to my own crazy and wonderful family for doing the same.

Thanks to Charlie Kochman for sitting by my side and encouraging me to dig deep and write the best books I can. Thanks to everyone at Abrams, especially Michael Jacobs, Jason Wells, Veronica Wasserman, Chad W. Beckerman, Susan Van Metre, Robby Imfeld, Alison Gervais, Elisa Garcia, Samantha Hoback, Kim Ku, and Michael Clark.

Thanks to Shaelyn Germain and Anna Cesary for all of the support and hard work. Thanks to Deb Sundin and the staff at An Unlikely Story for making book lovers happy every day.

Thanks to Rich Carr and Andrea Lucey for your support and friendship. Thanks to Paul Sennott and Ike Williams for your invaluable advice.

Thanks to Jess Brallier for cheering me on

year after year. Thanks to everyone at Poptropica for your support and inspiration.

Thanks to Sylvie Rabineau and Keith Fleer
for helping me navigate the film and TV
world. Thanks to everyone in Hollywood
who is working to bring new Wimpy Kid stories to life, including Nina Jacobson, Brad
Simpson, David Bowers, Elizabeth Gabler,
Roland Poindexter, Ralph Milero, and Van-
essa Morrison.

ABOUT THE AUTHOR

Jeff Kinney is a #1 *New York Times* bestselling author and a six-time Nickelodeon Kids' Choice Award winner for Favorite Book. Jeff has been named one of *Time* magazine's 100 Most Influential People in the World. He is also the creator of Poptropica, which was named one of *Time* magazine's 50 Best Websites. He spent his childhood in the Washington, D.C., area and moved to New England in 1995. Jeff lives with his wife and two sons in Massachusetts, where they own a bookstore, An Unlikely Story.